To Jasper and Kaia -
Think big!
Cousin Tom

A GIANT MAN from a TINY TOWN

A Story of ANGUS MACASKILL

Tom Ryan

Story by TOM RYAN
Art by CHRISTOPHER HOYT

NIMBUS
PUBLISHING
— NIMBUS.CA —

Angus MacAskill wasn't always a giant.

In fact, he was once a small boy. No bigger than the other children in his village.

When Angus was still very young, his family left their home on the Scottish Hebrides.

As the ship sailed away from the only home he'd ever known, the island his family had called its own for many generations, Angus stared back from the deck of the boat. He wondered what awaited them on the other side of the ocean.

The voyage was long, and there were days when it felt like they would never see land again.

In the middle of all that water, staring at a wide and open sky, Angus felt like the tiniest thing in the whole world.

The days rolled by on the ocean, each one just like the last, until one morning...

The people on the ship saw land. Angus stood on the deck with his family, watching excitedly as they arrived at their new home: Cape Breton Island.

Angus and his family settled in to their new home. Cape Breton Island was beautiful, the people were friendly, and the MacAskills loved their farm that sat high above the water, looking down at the little town of St. Anns.

The MacAskills soon became an important part of the community. Angus went to school and made friends, and when he wasn't in the classroom he was working on the farm with his family. Whether ploughing fields, tending to livestock, or harvesting crops, every day was full, from sunrise to sunset.

As Angus got older, he began to grow bigger...

And bigger...

And bigger still.

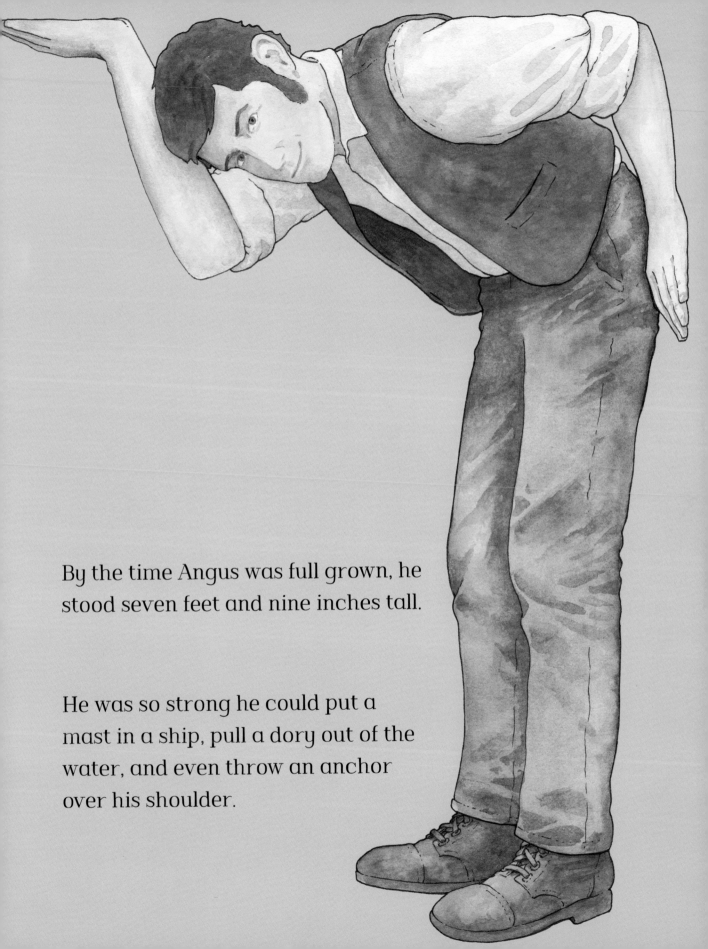

By the time Angus was full grown, he stood seven feet and nine inches tall.

He was so strong he could put a mast in a ship, pull a dory out of the water, and even throw an anchor over his shoulder.

Angus enjoyed hard work and was quick to help out anyone in need. For this, the townspeople loved him.

And Angus loved his Cape Breton home. He loved the changing seasons, the falling leaves, the drifting snow, and the sound of the fiddle as it drifted through the air on the warm summer breeze.

But even though he loved his little town, Angus knew there was a wider world beyond it.

He wondered if a man as big as he might find a better fit somewhere else.

One fine summer morning, Angus said goodbye to his family and his many friends and set off to find his fortune.

It wasn't hard for a man as large as Angus to get noticed....

And it wasn't long before he realized that other people stood out in the crowd as well, for many different reasons.

With his new friends, Angus travelled to many new places

And saw many new things.

Everywhere Angus went, even the grandest of people wanted to meet him. People were amazed by his height, his strength, and the space that he filled.

Even the hugest of rooms felt a little bit smaller when he walked through the door. And even in the largest crowds, in the biggest cities in the world, Angus stood taller than every person in sight.

Sometimes it felt like the eyes of the whole world were upon him.

But oddly enough, he found that the attention
didn't make him feel big at all.

In fact, in the middle of all those people,
Angus sometimes felt like the tiniest thing in
the world.

With each passing day, and each passing year, Angus
found himself thinking more and more about home.

In his tiny town, he'd been the biggest man around, but people had known him for who he was rather than how tall he stood.

He longed to see his family. He wished he could sit with his friends beneath the stars, listening to the fiddle and smelling the salt breeze drifting in from the sea.

Finally, Angus made a decision.

He packed his clothes and the mementos of his travels in his giant suitcase, and he said goodbye to his new friends.

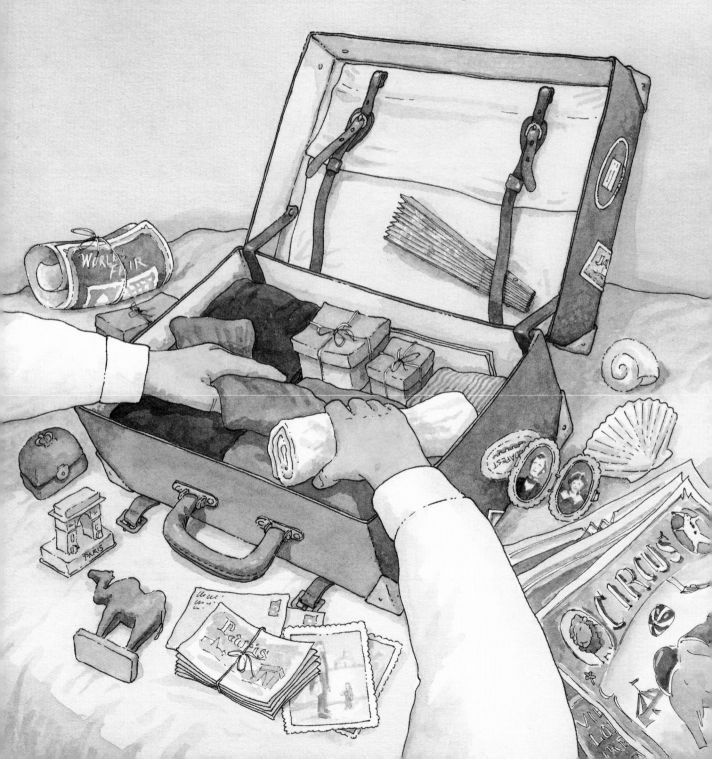

Angus had seen the world, and it was as wide and
wonderful as he'd always imagined.

But even a giant needs a place to call home.

About ANGUS MACASKILL

Angus MacAskill, also known as the Cape Breton Giant, was born in the Scottish Hebrides in 1825, and emigrated to Cape Breton with his family when he was still a young boy. By all accounts, he was normally proportioned until adolescence, when he began to grow rapidly, eventually reaching a full height of 7 feet, 9 inches.

As a young man, MacAskill joined P.T. Barnum's circus, and travelled throughout the West Indies and Cuba, Europe, and North America, often appearing alongside

ANGUS MacASKILL and TOM THUMB

General Tom Thumb. One story claims that while on tour in the United Kingdom, MacAskill was presented to Queen Victoria at Windsor Castle, who declared him "the tallest, stoutest and strongest man to ever enter the palace."

Angus MacAskill eventually chose to leave his show business career and return St. Anns on his beloved Cape Breton Island, where he ran several businesses successfully. He died peacefully in 1863, surrounded by many of his Cape Breton friends and neighbours.

For Frank and Virginia, who bring the magic
of Cape Breton to life.–TR

For my father, Murray, who was always
the giant in my life.–CH

Nimbus Publishing Limited
3660 Strawberry Hill St, Halifax, NS B3K 5A9
(902) 455-4286 nimbus.ca

Printed and bound in Canada
NB1280
Design: Heather Bryan
Photo of Angus MacAskill: Library and Archives Canada

Library and Archives Canada Cataloguing in Publication
      Ryan, Tom, 1977 February 26-, author
      A giant man from a tiny town : a story of Angus MacAskill / story by
      Tom Ryan ; art by Christopher Hoyt.
      Issued in print and electronic formats.
      ISBN 978-1-77108-654-7 (hardcover).
      —ISBN 978-1-77108-655-4 (HTML)

1. McAskill, Angus, 1825-1863—Juvenile fiction. 2. Giants—Nova Scotia—Cape Breton Island—Juvenile fiction.
3. Strong men—Nova Scotia—Cape Breton Island—Juvenile fiction. I. Hoyt, Christopher, illustrator II. Title.
PS8635.Y359G53 2018   jC813'.6   C2018-902856-4
                    C2018-902857-2

Nimbus Publishing acknowledges the financial support for its publishing activities from the Government of Canada, Canada Council for the Arts, and from the Province of Nova Scotia. We are pleased to work in partnership with the Province of Nova Scotia to develop and promote our creative industries for the benefit of all Nova Scotians.